Did Heaven Begin at 2:27?

A MEMOIR ABOUT SIGNS FROM MY BROTHER

By

Carolyn Koechlin Homer

Published by:
Wildebeest Publishing Company, LLC
Syracuse, New York

Do you have a story to tell? What's your animal spirit? Share it with us. #hellobeesties
Copyright © 2024 by Carolyn Koechlin Homer

Wildebeest
Publishing Co.

Wildebeest Publishing Company, LLC
All rights reserved, including the right to reproduce this book or portions thereof in any form.
Unauthorized copying or distribution of the book is forbidden.

For more information about copyrights and usage, special discounts on bulk purchases,
workshops, and engagements, please contact Wildebeest Publishing Company, LLC at
(315) 220-0217, info@wildebeestpublishing.com, or online at www.wildebeestpublishing.com
Wildebeest Publishing is dedicated to providing flexible remote work opportunities and has a
presence in Syracuse, New York City, and Tampa

Wildebeest Publishing Company, LLC paperback First Edition December 2024, United States
of America

Photographs used with permission by owners
Cover photo by Teresa Nora Trobbe
Author headshot by Thee Photo Ninja

ISBN 978-1-958233-40-5 (paperback)
LLCN 2024925659

Dedication

This book is dedicated to my sister-in-law, Nilufer Koechlin, for sharing
the police report. That one detail in the report changed my
outlook on life. I hope that it helps others to see this
world and beyond in a new and comforting way.

This book is also dedicated to Dad and Mom for giving us the
best childhood. Your legacy will live on through all of us.

Table of Contents

CHAPTER 1

Why Did I Write This Book?

I HAVE KNOWN for almost 12 years that I should be writing this book. However, I will admit that I have been a little intimidated and overwhelmed by the idea. Decades ago, my brother Bob used to mention how he was writing a book. This was before Amazon was a company and anyone could self-publish. I thought it was very bold and ambitious of him. I never knew what the book was about but looked forward to reading it one day. On November 24, 2012, Bob passed in an accident while cycling in Truckee, California. I will explain more about that soon. Due to this incident, I will likely never know about Bob's book; perhaps I can write a new one for him? That is a crazy concept to wrap my head around. It might not be related to the book that he was writing while here on earth, but my book is definitely being written with his help. He shall be my "ghost writer." This is a true story about what happened when he died. My intuition is my guide. It is telling me that the world needs to hear about it because dying can be a beautiful event, even in the worst of earthly circumstances. I wrote this book with the purpose of offering hope, in this world of sad statistics, to everyone on the planet.

While in year 11 of putting off writing this book, I was working in operations at a company in my hometown. Although I do love a good Excel spreadsheet, I would often dream about carving out quiet time to let my thoughts flow to tell this story. Being at home, I allowed routine distractions to block my quiet time. I knew that I should be prioritizing this book. However, I was not.

At the end of a work day in November of 2023, I went to get coffee. While returning to my desk, I recall asking myself if I should walk directly to my desk or if I should take a quick, indirect route so that I could say hello to a few colleagues. While walking by two colleagues, Estella and Victor, Estella said, "Maybe Carolyn will know." "What are you guys talking about?" I said. "What happens when we die?" Estella playfully asked. "Oh, I know! I mean, no one knows for sure, but I feel in my gut that I know. My brother told me when he died. I mean, he did not tell me directly, but he did. Everything is more than ok when we go." I then told them the story about what happened when my brother passed. Estella later came by my desk and said, "How did you know to walk by my desk when Victor and I were talking about that?" I told her that I didn't and that incidents like that sometimes happen now that my brother is gone.

A few weeks later, I was laid off from my position at that company. The work distraction was no longer an excuse. It was time to write this book. I hopped into my Jeep and drove eight hours from our hometown of Dunedin, Florida to our sister's house in Atlanta, Georgia, to make myself get this done. Wish me luck explaining something that I find difficult to put into words.

The second that my older brother Bob died in a cycling accident, my perspective on life changed. He oftentimes forgot birthdays and things like that. So, it is ironic that this last gift of his was the greatest one that I had ever received. I feel that it is part of my purpose to share this gift with you, as it was meant for all of us to hear. He once told me that he was writing a book. I do not believe that he ever finished writing it. I don't even know what the topic was. However, he used to mention to me that he was writing one. I like to think that he was able to finally become an author with my help through this book. Thank you, Bobby!

I do believe that after we pass, we become very knowledgeable about life's purpose. I feel that Bob has lovingly attempted to enlighten my family about this since his passing. I do not think that it would be right of me to keep this to myself. I also think that his new way of communicating with us is totally awesome and something that all survivors of loved ones who have passed should have the ability to experience.

Some say that they do not ever see signs of loved ones after they pass. Is it that messages are not being sent or that they are not being received? Of course, it could be both. I tend to think that if we are silent and genuinely looking for signs (even to the point that we verbally ask for them aloud), we will eventually receive a response. **Thus, another purpose in writing this book is to help you to find signs from your loved ones in heaven.** I know that it sounds bizarre, but I do believe it is possible. It has taken me 12 years of witnessing my older brother's signs and a break in my work schedule to finally sit down and write this book. I hope that you will enjoy it.

CHAPTER 2

What About Bob?

Growing Up Koechlin (Kentucky, Florida)   1977 – 1982

I WAS THE 4th child of 5 to be born to Bob and Sue Koechlin. Our order was
Kathleen (1966), Bob (1967), Mary (1969), me (7 years later in 1977), and Matt
(about 5 years later in 1981). I am pretty sure that my entry into the world was a
surprise to the entire family. Being that Bob was 10 years older than me, I do not
recall my first few years with him. I was born in Kentucky. At about four years

of age, our family moved to Florida due to our father's job promotion. This is where my memories overall first began.

We were a traditional middle-class family. Our dad was the breadwinner. Dad was from a German and Irish background and was the younger of two boys. His parents had him later in life, and then my parents had me later in life. (I recently found out that my paternal grandfather was in World War I and would be close to 130 years old if he were still alive?!) Our dad and his parents had a good sense of humor. Although my paternal grandpa had passed before I was born, I have evidence of this. I believe that Bobby inherited this trait.

My evidence lies in a story that my dad loves to tell. As I write this book, Dad is in his late 80s. When he tells this story, I see an 18 year old lighting up. Dad attended Xavier University, which was an all-male Catholic college. The University of Cincinnati was their rival football team. Xavier was the underdog at an away football game that Dad attended in 1956. When Xavier won that game, my dad and his buddies rushed the field. My mom dislikes the next part of this story because she does not believe that it would have been possible. However, Dad says that one of the field rushers then took a club from a cop, bopped him in the head to distract him, and then Dad and his buddies proceeded to pull the goalpost out of the ground. They then carried it on its side from the University of Cincinnati to Xavier. The further they got with the pole, the smaller the group became. "People started dropping off to go to bars" is how the story goes.

Our dad was one of the few to keep the pace. The next thing they knew, they were at Xavier ... with an enormous goalpost. They buried it in the leaves at the baseball stadium. Then what? Part of it was placed outside of their dorm to pose as a downspout. Apparently, back then, you had a container that each student had to send laundry home and back. Our paternal grandfather smuggled a saw into that container so that Dad could chop up the goalpost into manageable pieces for the guys to each have as a keepsake, a trophy to put on display as evidence of their bravery and football victory. Dad then returned a chunk of post back in the "laundry container" for Grandpa to engrave. I am now the proud owner of this piece. Grandpa placed it on a walnut base (so fancy) and engraved it to read, "1956 FOOT-BALL [he used a dash] XU-UC." I think that story speaks volumes regarding where Bobby and a few of the rest of us may have inherited our wit.

Dad left Xavier to attend St. Joseph's Abbey, a monastery in Spencer, Massachusetts, for a few years and then returned to Xavier to finish up a psychology degree. He taught science/biology for many years. He then earned a master's degree in radiation biology at St. Mary's College in Winona, Minnesota, (sponsored by the National Science Foundation) while living in Cincinnati and having the first three kids. Uncle Tom helped to introduce him to General Electric when the teaching income became a challenge with three kids at home. After receiving a promotion, GE transferred the family to Pittsburgh for two years. Then, he earned another promotion, which landed us in Louisville for my birth. Dad worked in sales at GE. Sales is what Bobby ended up going into as well. Dad was in about 12 weddings and had a great network of friends. This trait translated well into his sales career.

Mom came from a German and Irish background. She was the oldest of 5 siblings and was her high school Homecoming Queen. Her two sisters were as well. She sang in the church choir and played the piano. She attended the all-female college near Xavier, Edgecliff, also known as Our Lady of Cincinnati, studying education. I do not have any mischievous stories about Mom. Many of us believe she is a saint. She was always volunteering and remembering all 5 of us (and later our children) for all of our birthdays, first communions, graduations, et cetera.

The story goes that most of the students had left campus one summer. Mom, however, was still in town. Dad needed a date for an event, so he asked Mom. The initials of Mom's university were OLC, which the guys sometimes referred to as Our Last Chance. Mom jokes that the guys preferred to date the gals at the nursing school. Dad's last chance turned into a 59 year marriage with many adventures.

Halloween in Louisville, Kentucky
Bob is on the far right and dressed as Evel Knievel, a motorcycle stunt
performer and entertainer. As I write this book, I learn that Evel passed
away a few minutes from me in 2007 in Clearwater, Florida

So, there we were in Louisville, Kentucky. I was four years old. All I remember from Louisville is rolling down the stairs of our two-story house, breaking
a glass jewelry holder that I could access from my crib (because I wanted out),
watching Princess Diana's wedding on a fat TV, competing for TV time with my
siblings (I wanted to watch the Pink Panther and had to pry my teenage sisters
away from episodes of General Hospital), an occasional snow storm, crashing
my sister Mary's slumber parties, and wearing my mom's slips and carrying her
fancy purses like I was going to prom. Bobby was around, but I do not remember
much about him in those years. I DO remember my dad telling us that he earned
another promotion, which meant that all seven of us were flying to Dunedin,
Florida. Matt had just been born. My mom must have been so overwhelmed.
"You will know that we are there when you see palm trees," is something that

I remember Dad saying. Four decades later, I see palm trees almost daily, and I love it.

Bob in High School (Florida)   1982 – 1985

Robert Koechlin, Jr. and Sue Ceraolo Pickles

Have you ever seen *The Wonder Years*? One of the characters was named, Paul. In his early high school years, Bobby reminded me of Paul. Ever since the age of four, Bobby had some thick glasses. He also had teeth screaming for braces. Even though he was Paul from *The Wonder Years*, I am told that he was always fun and popular. The facade turning point story I recall is that one special gal in high school had a vision for my brother. She influenced him to get contacts and braces. He owes Stephanie, to say the least. After his passing, I posted a few photos of Bob pre-Stephanie, and his California friends were in disbelief. So much of his high school days, he was loving his new look.

Siblings before Matt was born

In elementary school, and really throughout all of life, I always felt older than I was because I had three siblings in their teens in the 80s. I remember going to kindergarten and having to work around two teenage sisters spraying Aqua Net in the one bathroom that the 5 of us kids shared. We think that this is why Bob was so patient with women later in life. Our house was approximately 1,800 square feet. Our father purchased it knowing that he would have three college kids living out of the house within about 5 years. Thus, for a few solid years, we all learned to live closely. I shared a room with the baby brother at first and eventually got my own room when Kathleen went away to the University of Florida (UF).

My other memories from my time living with Bob and the rest of the family involved playing in the neighborhood with the many kids my age whenever we had free time and coming home for dinner when we heard our father ring the enormous train bell in our backyard. (He had inherited it from his father, who worked on the B & O Railroad.) Meanwhile, my older siblings were busy living through high school. They all attended Clearwater Central Catholic High School (CCC) at the same time. My parents had so many tuition bills, orthodontist bills, optical bills (we were all pretty blind), and soon-to-be college bills. Kudos to Bob and Sue for tolerating all of this!

Bob and Kath did not seem to bond too much. I do recall them walking on stilts and riding a unicycle around our neighborhood's cul-de-sac. Bob was a popular guy (Prom King 1985, baby!), which seemed to sometimes bother Kathleen. He was even perceived to have been the favorite child of my mother. Whether this was true or not, it did not bother the rest of us.

I remember Bob getting a (or the very first) job cutting grass on Clearwater Beach. This involved the entire family piling into the brown and white station wagon with the lawn mower on top. Why would an entire family be needed to mow a lawn with one lawn mower? We had to accompany the favorite, I suppose. Bob was also a waiter at a Spanish restaurant in town (Casa Gallardo?), where he once spilled something on a customer … who later gave him a $20 tip. This was the 80s, so $20 was pretty huge. The irony! Bob's personality got him out of a lot of trouble.

My dad recently told a story about Bob always having either really good or really bad timing. Dad focused on the bad timing for one of his favorite tales of Bob in high school. Picture it: Dunedin, 1980 something (said like Sophia from *The Golden Girls*). My parents really never left us home alone. I cannot blame them. They needed and deserved a break at times. Trane was having some type of trip to honor their team, so my folks left Dunedin (Trane was purchased by GE). They left their teenagers in Dunedin for this trip. I forget where I went that weekend, but Bob took full advantage and had a party. From what I recall, the party remained under control. As my dad recalls, he came home to a spotless house. My dad got out of his car shortly after returning from the Trane trip and heard something crunch under his shoe. He looked down and saw "Beam." The Jim got away, but my dad knew that logo and was onto the case. As time went on, my parents found random things, such as empty beer cans, under the couch cushions. The cuckoo clock lost its koo. What had happened in Dunedin while Mom and Dad were away trying to get away from it all?

Dad was sometimes direct but mostly indirect. Instead of confronting Bob Junior, he placed all of the evidence in places that Bob would be sure to find. Dad would rely on good ole Catholic guilt, partly as punishment and mainly as entertainment. Dad placed beer cans in Bob's pillowcase and even in the "kids" toilet. Somehow, Jr. and Sr. ended up talking it out. When dad asked Bobby where all of the garbage went, Bob said that they contained it and dumped it at the hardware store behind our house. Dad then taught Bobby about dumpsters and the law. Never a dull moment

Another memory where Bob had bad timing was when my dad was driving along 580. He looked over at Kash n' Karry, where Bob worked. What are the odds that my dad would be stopped at a light on 580 just as Bob was loading beer into the trunk of his car? Again, instead of asking Bob directly about the beer, my dad waited until everyone was home. While Bob was in the kitchen at home, Dad brought up needing to get something from the trunk of Bob's car. "Oh, I'll get it." is what Dad recalls Bobby saying. I forget how that story ended, but Dad loved getting those reactions. Good grief.

Bob in College (Florida)   1985 – 1990

Bob and his Delta Tau Delta lifelong fraternity brothers with the legendary Mr. Two Bits (in the tie) at a University of Florida football game … Like our grandma used to say: "You oughta Google him in" if you have not heard of Mr. Two Bits.

Ready for the next steps, Bob applied and was accepted into the University of Florida. During his summers, he would work masonry/construction with his friend D'Arcy Bellamy. I think that he was saving up for a motorcycle because other memories involve him driving me around town on the back of a Kawasaki Ninja. After his Ninja days, he once left his WALLET on top of his car before taking off. The person driving behind him somehow gathered all of his belongings that had flown toward their car AND RETURNED THEM TO HIM. Bob's luck was unusual. It is like he always knew that someone was looking out for him.

Having older siblings in our house was like living with celebrities. I so looked up to all three of them. Being the only older male sibling, Bob was especially fun when I had my friends over. He would let us play on his car, tell jokes, and kind of show off to them. I beamed with pride, putting him on display like we were having a Show-and-Tell day at school.

The bottom of a letter from our sister Kathleen to the family referencing Bob and his Ninja motorcycle during the college years at UF

One of Bob's letters to the family from UF explaining typical fraternity shenanigans

It was the 1980s, and I was in *Bop Magazine's* target market. I was mainly a very large groupie of the New Kids on the Block. However, Debbie Gibson and Kirk Cameron were also big in my world. I had a friend whose mom would take us to all of the concerts we could attend (Thank you, Nancy!). When Debbie Gibson came to Tampa, we were there. We were there with big hair, DG shirts, and those ginormous buttons of Debbie. (I recall the buttons having a diameter of about 6 inches.) I had a pink camera that used film. I would snap a photo and then wind up the film a few times in preparation for the next photo. When it was time to develop the film, I usually bought "doubles" and hoped for the best. Many times, I paid for photos of the ground, and the like, that were worthless. Being able to delete photos prior to developing them was not an option. Waiting for my film to be developed was sometimes as exciting to me as Christmas Day.

You can imagine my excitement when Bob said that he would take me to the mall to pick up my photos of the Debbie Gibson concert. Our mode of transportation was his Kawasaki Ninja motorcycle. So, I was in middle school, buying my photos of Debbie with the help of my celebrity-status (in my mind) brother on his motorcycle. We were the stars of State Road 580 for a total of probably 20 minutes. It is one of my favorite memories of Bobby and one that I spoke of during his funeral.

A tale that I recall from Bob's college days involved him being the Keg Chairman, or some similarly grand title, of Delta Tau Delta (DTD). He did his job so well that his grades slipped. He said that after the grades suffered, he had to meet at UF's Administration building with the goal of talking the Dean (or the powers that be) into giving him a second chance. He asked if he could get this second chance, and if he was able to get good grades, could he stay enrolled? The Dean agreed. Bob told me that while walking out of that meeting, he realized that he should probably become a salesman. He did end up getting good grades and eventually graduating from UF with a bachelor's degree in marketing. As mentioned previously, he did indeed pursue a career in sales.

One very significant summer job that Bob had was with Southwestern Books. He took the job with a few of his fraternity brothers. It was where he was really able to perfect his sales techniques. This was before the internet, so people were still buying those A-Z encyclopedia sets for their homes. The sets were hilariously enormous. My parents had one. I believe that they purchased the set with a custom, two-tiered shelving system.

Bob and his friends were trained by the book company to convince someone to let them live with them for the summer. I am not sure if rent was involved. However, I do remember Bob and his friends living with a priest at some point. We would receive hand-written letters from him detailing the adventures of Bob the Book Man. After Bob's passing, his fraternity brother Tony Carulli, who lived through the Southwestern Books summer with him, mentioned that one time, the two of them were traveling on the highway. Bob was reading the paper in the passenger seat. A large freight truck ran them off of the road. Tony pulled off to the side of the road so quickly that their car did a 90-degree fall on its side. Tony recalled that shift and that Bob still had the newspaper opened and in his hands when they landed on their sides. They walked away basically unscathed. Was someone watching out for them yet again there?

Bob the Bachelor Pre-Nilufer
(FL, Mass, Wash)   1990 – 1998

The experience in sales helped him to then become Bacardi Bob. He landed a job after college selling Bacardi to establishments in South Florida. This led to his promotions in Worcester, Massachusetts and Seattle, Washington. Bob loved adventures. During this chapter of life, he was also getting a pilot's license, running with bulls in Spain, journaling, cycling and skiing black diamonds. The cloudy weather in Seattle was a bit too depressing for Bob, so he decided to move to sunny Californ – i – a.

Bob the Husband & Father (California)   1999 – 2012

It was 1999, the Dot-com era, which was kind of like a digital gold rush. Bob was eager to participate in the action and began working for a company then called exp.com. Bob likely had no idea that a company called "Google" was also doing what he was doing.

The customer would go to the exp.com site to ask any questions. The site would then locate an expert to answer that question. The service's sophistication was somewhere between using the Southwestern encyclopedias and searching on the aforementioned Google (which was then simultaneously in its infancy).

Before I explain the mission of exp.com, I will explain what an encyclopedia is to the younger readers. An encyclopedia set involved approximately 26 matching books. Each book had a letter on its spine. The A book contained information related to the most important A words and so forth. This sounds pretty hilarious to me, looking back on this "technology." If someone needed information from an encyclopedia, they had to walk over to the giant set of 26 books, pull out the book with the letter that corresponded to the main word being researched, and flip to the section of that book involving the word ... If that word was even in the book. My mom had a special encyclopedia bookshelf that fit all of our books A-Z. I am not sure how often we "upgraded" our books. It must have been expensive for the upgrade.

Back to the year 2000. Bob was working for exp.com. The world now no longer had to rely on encyclopedias. Let's say that I was researching alligators. I could go to exp.com, type in my question(s), and pay a small fee (I recall it being a few dollars per question.). Exp.com would then FIND AN EXPERT in alligators and have them reply. This is how I remember it. My mom wanted to be supportive of her son and would ask questions regularly. There evidently were not enough moms out there to keep the company going, and they eventually closed. Eventually, Google took over that space.

1999 was also the year when Bob started dating a girl named Nilufer. I was working in downtown Tampa when he told me about her on a phone call one evening after work. He explained her name to me as "just like the Persian form for Jennifer." Nilufer was raised in the San Francisco area and met Bob on a ski trip. They married in 2001 and had Baby Kiana in 2008. Our daughter was born in 2005, so it was cool to me that our girls would get to grow up together on opposite sides of the US. Our daughter could set an example for Kiana just like Bob had done for me in my youth. Good or bad, he did set an example (and was somehow my Confirmation sponsor when I was in 8th grade).

EXP.COM
(a poem for Bob Koechlin Jr. sung to the tune of the Little Drummer Boy song)

Sign up Bob told me
Exp.com
Its a new company
Exp.com
A way to make money
Exp.com
For the whole family
Exp.com
Just ask his Mom
She thinks its Da Bomb

There's plenty to advise
Exp.com
Pretend that you are wise
Exp.com
Don't look them in the eyes
Exp.com
Cause they might realize
Your advise is wrong
Cause you're really dumb
Exp.com

Dad got a hit one day
Exp.com
But didn't make them pay
Exp.com
What is the point you say?
Exp.com
He had fun anyway
Exp.com
He helped out his son
By just signing on

Carna was asked advice
Exp.com
She answered really nice
Exp.com
Got paid her asking price
Exp.com
Then paid back the invoice
Cause it was her Mom
Just playing for fun
on Exp.com

Copyright: #1Hits by MTK 12/99

A poem that our sister, Mary, wrote in 1999—Mary was our
family's songwriter in a "Weird Al" Yankovic kind of way.

rkoechlin@exp.com
www.exp.com/4.htm
650 330 9044 direct

1374 Willow Road
Menlo Park, CA 94025
650 566 0380 main
650 566 0382 fax

the expert experience

ROBERT KOECHLIN

Inside Sales Representative

CHAPTER 3

The 1ˢᵗ Sign: November 24, 2012

BOB LOVED CYCLING. He had many Persian relatives in California who would visit on Sundays. We joked about Bob not understanding Farsi and that his bike rides offered him some relief when these family gatherings became overwhelming for him. He had a background in sharing a bathroom in the 1980s with two sisters that involved the three of them getting ready for high school and Bob's eyes dodging them and their Aqua Net hairspray. This may have prepared him for Nilufer's many sisters and other family members visiting their home weekly. Although it was a blessing, Bob sometimes let the in-laws have the house and went biking as he was a rookie at speaking Farsi.

The University of Florida Gators of Gainesville, Florida, have a tradition of playing the Florida State Seminoles of Tallahassee, Florida, every post-Thanksgiving Saturday. Bob, Nilufer, and Kiana had hosted Thanksgiving of 2012 at their home in Lake Tahoe. About 48 hours had passed since Thanksgiving Day, and the family members were dissipating/departing for their respective homes. Thus, Bob left for his typical bike ride. The date was November 24, 2012. Bob and Nilufer's four-year-old daughter, Kiana, went down for a nap. Bob set up the hot tub and popped in his earbuds for this bike ride.

When Nilufer, felt that he had been gone on his trip too long, she began to worry and called the authorities to begin searching for him. Surprisingly, the man on the other end of the phone said that he would be at their Tahoe home in 10 minutes. When the gentleman showed up, he informed her in a supportive manner and then handed Nilufer two Cliff Bars, his jacket, his wallet, and his wedding ring. Nilufer fell to the floor in agony while Kiana continued her rarely-taken afternoon nap.

Based on a portion of the accident's police report, we now know that Bob approached a roundabout that afternoon on his bike ride where a commercial grade Ram 2500 did not see him and unfortunately took his life. A few witnesses, including a doctor who stopped to help with CPR, tried to salvage what they could. A hospital was located across the street from the roundabout. Nevertheless, he was not able to make it that far.

Bob passed away participating in a hobby that he had loved his entire life. If he had survived, he would have very likely been disabled, depressed, or his spirit stifled in some fashion. Because the passing seemed to be instant, I am at peace with knowing that he very likely did not suffer.

Meanwhile, over in Florida, I had fallen asleep in the bottom of our daughter's bunk bed that night after saying prayers. At around 10:00 pm, my husband came into the room and told me to get up because my parents kept leaving messages on the answering machine. (About one year later, I would surrender the landline and answering machine, but I do still have my parents' voicemail messages saved on it. I doubt that I will ever listen to those calls again. For some reason, I cannot erase them or trash that machine.) I also noticed a text on my cell from my younger brother Matt that said, "Call Mom and Dad now." I called my parents, but the line was busy. They were updating our oldest sister, Kathleen. Then Matt called. He told me to put my husband on the phone because he did not want to tell me directly. I could tell that someone had died. I figured it was our Grandmother, who was 92. No one in our family had passed before that day. Thus, what I was about to experience was a completely new feeling and perspective. My breathing picked up the pace as I listened. My husband had been playing video games in our guest room. The only light in the room came from the computer screen. I took a seat on the floor of the dark room and listened to the news. "Matt, cut to the chase," Chris said. "Bobby?" I heard next. Chris ended the call, gave me a hug on the ground, and said, "It's Bobby. He died." Bam.

Our sweet parents took off for California the next morning at 8:30 am. When I pulled up to their house, I saw our father pacing in the front yard. I drove them to the airport with both of them sitting behind me. I remember my mom taking a call before we left their Florida driveway. A neighbor who had moved just outside of Dunedin, who was our mom's oldest and closest friend, had called. Mom had to tell her that her little boy was gone. My mom is not an emotional person at all, but I could hear her voice shaking as she told her. In my 35 years of living, it was one of the only times that I heard my mom's voice quiver with tears. It was so sad.

On November 29, 2012, a kind neighbor of mine dropped me off at the Tampa airport so that I could meet my sister Mary in Atlanta. We then flew out together from there. Our father, brother Matt, and sister Kathleen arrived ahead of us and were able to attend the cremation event. Our father bravely saw Bob's remains one last time that day. He read a letter from Nilufer to Bob. Nilufer's mom and niece also saw Bob separately that day. Unfortunately, Mary and I intended to go but did not land in time. Bob probably figured that we would be too emotional and wanted none of it.

We were all flying by the seat of our pants, unsure of proper protocol, making things up as we went. No one in our family had ever passed away before in four generations within the 35 years that I had been alive. The stress level was high, causing a few of us to barely dodge accidents on the California roads that were foreign to us. However, we survived.

Upon arrival at Bob and Nilufer's house in California, we were greeted with warmth. Persian food abounded. Many visitors stopped by the house to visit. My mom's four siblings were even all able to make it. They flew to California from Michigan, Ohio, Virginia, and Tennessee. A few of my cousins were there as well. If you are ever unsure of what to do for a friend when they lose a friend or family member, reach out and just talk. Every visitor, card, sentimental gift, and hug was remembered and appreciated.

Bob's funeral service on Sunday, December 2, 2012, was more like a wedding and wedding reception. I sat in the front row of the chapel with my siblings, parents, and other relatives. Attendees were on the floor in front of us. All of the pews were filled. People were also standing around the perimeter of the rows and appeared on the upper deck of the chapel as well. A few patient and understanding friends stood outside just to listen to the service. There were flowers, a slide show, food, hotel room blocks, a memorial website, and other elements indicative of a celebration. Attendees wore colorful clothing and told many humorous stories, just as we imagined Bob would have liked. Weeks before I knew my brother was living out his last few days, I found a fun blue dress with pockets. It was cobalt blue (also known as Florida Gator blue). I did not have much extra cash but bought it anyway. As I packed it for the funeral, I suspected that God led me to it for this purpose. When scrambling to pack, I remember not knowing if that dress would be appropriate but also feeling like Bob would guide us even in this department. The family got ready and gathered for the service. My two sisters and my sister-in-law were all wearing the exact same color. Coincidence?

The eulogies were meaningful, caring, and even humorous. They were told by Nilufer, our father, co-workers, neighbors (including children), cycling friends, the best man from their wedding, myself, and other loved ones. People came from Washington, Ohio, Tennessee, Texas, Georgia, Massachusetts, Florida, other parts of California, and beyond. Our brave Father, who had just voluntarily seen Bob's remains the day prior, read the poem "The Dash" by Linda Ellis. If you have not read this powerful and brief poem, I highly recommend it as it gives one great perspective on life. I have it hanging in my office on the wall and also at the bottom of my paper inbox. When I get to the bottom of my papers, I am reminded of my overall purpose in life. It helps me to avoid sweating the small stuff.

"The Dash" speaks of the line that is between one's birth date and date of death. It reminds us to be wise regarding how we spend our days between the starting and finish line. It mentions how many of us focus on materialistic things during our time but that those materialistic things cannot be taken with us when we pass. In Florida, at the time of writing this book, we just survived two hurricanes. The first hurricane grazed our coast and flooded many homes. Many of our friends scrambled to clean their homes to avoid mold growth and further damage. On every street along the coast, passersby got a glimpse of each homeowner's possessions: bed mattresses, carpet, bags of clothes, drywall, trim, toys, couches, old ruined photo albums of cherished memories. It was very sad but also a good reminder to us all to make the most of our hyphenated days. What are we focused on while we are here? Many neighbors helped neighbors, even ones they had not met yet, with cleanup, which inspired a much-needed renewal of our sense of community here in Florida.

After the funeral, we walked across the street for the "reception." There were 300+ people in attendance. Scotch was Bobby's favorite drink and was served until it was gone. The evening ended ironically with a small dance party involving Kiana. We could all feel Bobby smiling down on all of us. One friend said that Bob "got a run for his money" through his life on Earth. Hopefully, he can continue to help those of us who are still here to make the most of our lives, too.

As I left California, I remember thinking that I probably would not see Nilufer before she met someone new. She resembled JLo and was a newly single mom to a precious 4-year-old girl. I knew that Bob would want her to be happy. Thus, I told her that I knew that it was really early to be talking about it, but for whatever it was worth, she had my blessing to move on eventually. If I were her, I would want some kind of blessing. In the spirit of going with my gut, I gave the informal blessing.

Five months passed. Nilufer mustered up the courage and energy to make a copy of the accident's police report and send it to my parents. She understandably did not seem to want to read it. I, however, had to. I read every detail, I suppose as part of my healing process and for closure. It took me about 30 minutes to get through it. Every single detail was listed, including information about the remaining belongings. I was drawn to the part about Bob's iPod. It mentioned that the detective wiped the blood off of it to see that it was on **power save mode at 2:27 (2 minutes and 27 seconds) into the song by Styx called "Come Sail Away."**

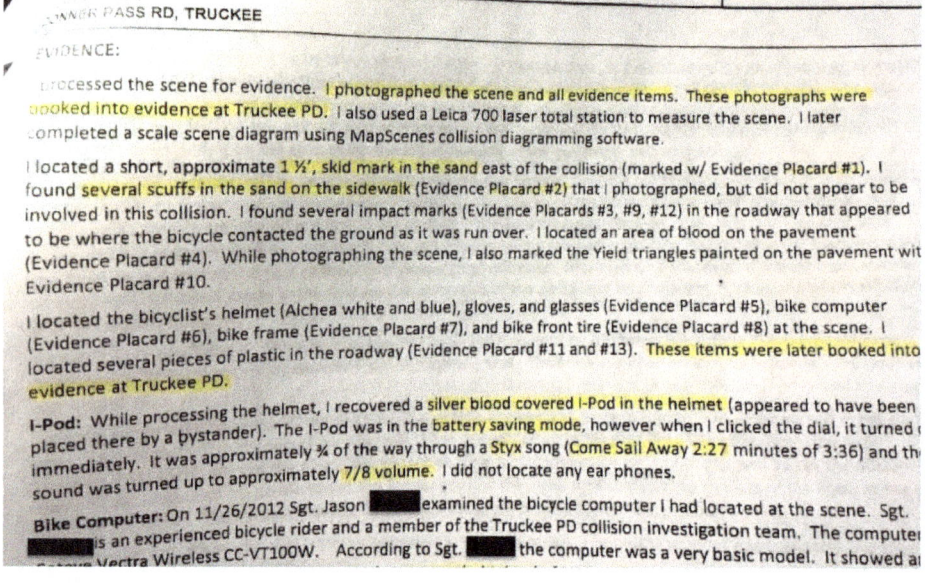

DONNER PASS RD, TRUCKEE

EVIDENCE:

processed the scene for evidence. I photographed the scene and all evidence items. These photographs were booked into evidence at Truckee PD. I also used a Leica 700 laser total station to measure the scene. I later completed a scale scene diagram using MapScenes collision diagramming software.

I located a short, approximate 1 ½', skid mark in the sand east of the collision (marked w/ Evidence Placard #1). I found several scuffs in the sand on the sidewalk (Evidence Placard #2) that I photographed, but did not appear to be involved in this collision. I found several impact marks (Evidence Placards #3, #9, #12) in the roadway that appeared to be where the bicycle contacted the ground as it was run over. I located an area of blood on the pavement (Evidence Placard #4). While photographing the scene, I also marked the Yield triangles painted on the pavement with Evidence Placard #10.

I located the bicyclist's helmet (Alchea white and blue), gloves, and glasses (Evidence Placard #5), bike computer (Evidence Placard #6), bike frame (Evidence Placard #7), and bike front tire (Evidence Placard #8) at the scene. I located several pieces of plastic in the roadway (Evidence Placard #11 and #13). These items were later booked into evidence at Truckee PD.

I-Pod: While processing the helmet, I recovered a silver blood covered I-Pod in the helmet (appeared to have been placed there by a bystander). The I-Pod was in the battery saving mode, however when I clicked the dial, it turned on immediately. It was approximately ¾ of the way through a Styx song (Come Sail Away 2:27 minutes of 3:36) and the sound was turned up to approximately 7/8 volume. I did not locate any ear phones.

Bike Computer: On 11/26/2012 Sgt. Jason ███ examined the bicycle computer I had located at the scene. Sgt. ███ is an experienced bicycle rider and a member of the Truckee PD collision investigation team. The computer ██████ Vectra Wireless CC-VT100W. According to Sgt. ███ the computer was a very basic model. It showed a

I have always loved numbers. In middle school, I would enter the math competitions after the school would recommend contestants. I took the SAT while in middle school. After getting an MBA and expecting our daughter, I decided to take a career detour and teach Algebra. I have just always loved numbers. When I read the police report comment about 2:27, I KNEW that meant something. This new sibling intuition is difficult to explain. I ran to my parents' computer, went to YouTube, and searched for *Styx "Come Sail Away" Lyrics*. I listened to the words as I watched the seconds tick on the screen. I noticed how the song began at a slow pace and mentioned reflecting on one's childhood.

The lyrics were:

"I'm sailing away set an open course for the virgin sea
I've got to be free free to face the life that's ahead of me
On board I'm the captain so climb aboard

We'll search for tomorrow on every shore
And I'll try oh Lord I'll try to carry on

I look to the sea reflections in the waves spark my memory
Some happy some sad
I think of childhood friends and the dreams we had
We live happily forever so the story goes
But somehow we missed out on that pot of gold
But we'll try best that we can to carry on..."

Then there were a few seconds of music without words. I watched the timer on the video. As it hit 2:27, I could not believe what I was hearing. It was so perfectly timed that it seemed like Bob had left a message for his survivors and friends. The music sped up at exactly 2:27, and then the lyrics read:

"...A gathering of angels appeared above my head
They sang to me this song of hope, and this is what they said
They said come sail away, come sail away
Come sail away with me"

It was one of the most memorable moments of my life. Was Bob trying to tell us something from the second he left us physically? I called Nilufer in California and asked her if I could reveal this portion of the police report to her. She agreed and then fell to her knees in the grocery store after hearing the good news. **How could I not share this information with others?**

A few things had to happen for this to have happened. Deduce what you will.

1. The iPod had to have avoided the impact of the truck.
2. The iPod had to have been on power save mode.
3. The detective had to have been precise enough to have written down the exact second of the song that was frozen.
4. Nilufer had to have been willing to have shared the police report with us.
5. My intuition had to have told me that this 2:27 meant something.

Since learning of this first sign from Bob, I have told others about it when opportunities present themselves. Friends and strangers alike (ex: a contractor working on our house) have had the same reaction. Most of them say that receiving the message gave them chills. They oftentimes will show me their arm so that I can see the physical hairs standing up straight. The even stranger phenomenon about this is that I sometimes shiver when telling this story. For many years, I have felt that I needed to share the message with others on a larger scale. I had wanted to write a book about it but found it difficult and overwhelming to begin putting my words on paper. Until the moment I realized that time on this planet is short and not a guarantee. If I did not take action, the message may evaporate after the passing of the next generation in my family. I also felt that "Big Brother" wanted me to deliver it for him to those on our side of life. When this same feeling was present during his first Valentine's Day away from us (see Chapter 5), everything went far better than expected. Thus, in January 2020, nearly 7 years after his passing, I began writing the outline for this book.

I have certainly had time to witness many more signs in these last 12 years and ponder their meaning. I hope that these chapters help to explain the unexplainable related to how Bob has continued to communicate with his friends and family members since his passing. Although I miss him, I do cherish this new communication method and feel like we chat more now than we ever did when he was physically here (especially with the 3-hour time difference from Florida to California). I hope that the readers of this book will be able to understand this concept and be open to seeing where their loved ones who have passed may be trying to catch their attention. It can be a beautiful gift if welcomed.

Our Final Sibling Photo in 2010—Bob was in town for his 25th CCC high school reunion. We rarely reunited, so this photo session had to be scheduled when we were all in the same house which happened to take place after Bob landed from California at about 10:00 pm.

Photo credit: Marcia Simmons Anderson

A new type of sibling photo taken at Bob's Celebration of Life in 2012—
We initially thought that it might be taken as being inappropriate.
Thankfully, his friends and family members seemed to appreciate it.

CHAPTER 4

The Number 5

THE HOUR THAT Bob passed, our family received the second sign. Bob and Nilufer had hosted Thanksgiving Day at their house in Lake Tahoe in 2012. I imagine that it was fun and very busy. The crowd died down, and the last one to leave for home was Bob's sister-in-law, Parvin. She pulled out of their driveway in her Prius and headed for her home. About an hour into her drive, she received the call from her little sister Nilufer to turn around because Bob had passed. Understandably, Parvin was in such a rush to comfort her sister that she left the door to her Prius open and ran back into the Tahoe home.

I am told that in this part of Lake Tahoe, the residents know that there are bears in the area. However, they rarely see the bears. It seems to be that way in Florida with alligators. Shortly after Parvin returned to the ski house, she and Nilufer looked outside to see a momma bear and her four cubs (note: 5 bears) going after a granola bar that Parvin had left in a jacket in the Prius. The bears were apparently very entertaining in that they tore up the leather, throwing part of the steering wheel outside of the car. One bear also used the car as a restroom (#2) during this incident. Nilufer and Parvin somehow were already able to see the comic relief in this situation, as Bob was a practical joker. When our older sister Mary found out about this, she, too, thought that this had something to do with Bob. Mary said, "He probably isn't used to using his new powers up there and is kinda misfiring." Parvin told that story at the funeral. I think that all of the attendees saw the humor in it. Her car was later totaled by the insurance company, and she was given a new Prius.

There were five children in our family. At this point, it was not obvious yet to me how Bob was going to continue using the number 5 through his signs and if this was the reason for the use of the number. I do recall when the light bulb first went off that the number 5 was beginning to be a heavenly Bob trend. Our sister Mary said that they had a board game that involved 5 Mickey Mouse pieces. One of the 5 pieces had been missing for a while before Bob passed. Thus, Mary's family replaced it with a rock. On December 7, 2012, a few weeks after Bobby's passing, Mary started cleaning the house to prepare for a visit from our parents. They had planned the visit before Bob passed and wanted to keep the plans in motion even though we had all just seen each other in California at the funeral. When Mary was almost finished tidying up, that fifth Mickey Mouse piece mysteriously appeared in the hallway. It had been missing in action during many rounds of playing the game. Coincidence?

The fourth and fifth children in our family were born in Kentucky. I do not really have memories of Kentucky, as we moved to Florida when I was four. However, I did notice something interesting about the Kentucky Derbies that followed Bob's passing. On 5/4/13, a horse named Orb won the race. I am not too comfortable talking about orbs. (I was the chaperone on the St. Augustine, Florida, field trip who begrudgingly attended the ghost tour, denied that orbs existed, and then saw many in the photos that I took that night.) Many bright, round objects have appeared in my photos when I was not looking for them (at the funeral, when with my family members since his passing, et cetera.) During the following year's Kentucky Derby, on 5/3/14, horse number 5, named California Chrome, won. Bob was a resident of California for many years before he passed, and there is that number 5 again. Coincidence?

CHAPTER 5

Valentine's Day 2013

CHRIS AND I married in 2002. I earned an MBA in 2003. After working in the sales/marketing world for two years and for the in-laws' family fly-fishing business for three years, I left the fly-fishing business for a new career in teaching. It was a change. Although, it made sense to me because we were finally expecting our daughter after 2.5 years of infertility. One of our fly-fishing customers told us that there was a demand for middle school math teachers. As mentioned previously, I love numbers and mathematics, and this career change would allow me to have summers off with our young daughter. The years 2004 – 2012 were my main teaching years. I loved the subject but did not have the gift of teaching to the masses. It was tough to deal with failure because I felt that I had excelled in almost everything up until that point in life. I was accepted into the college and sorority of my choice. I had a successful election as a Student Senator while at the University of Florida, and when I applied to almost all of my extracurricular activities (Student Government Cabinet, et cetera), my mission was accomplished. Upon graduating from UF, I had multiple job offers. My MBA courses were fun and overall successful. Then came teaching. What the heck? Why couldn't I teach? I taught at private schools while returning to school to earn a teaching certificate. The day after our parents' house burned down from a contractor's mistake, I successfully passed my teaching exam. I switched to public school, took a raise, and still did not love it. My understanding principal and I sat down several times to discuss it. Before the summer of 2012, I knew that I should return to the corporate world. I did not know then that I was about to lose my brother and that free time during my two-year sabbatical was going to be needed to accomplish many related tasks.

One weekday in February of 2013, I took a yoga class at the YMCA. I always feel the most at peace during the end of a yoga or pilates session (where the instructor lets the class lay on their sides and pretty much fall asleep.) During this part of class, all I can say is that I had a flashback to our wedding day. I saw my husband's Kappa Alpha (KA) fraternity brothers surrounding me at the reception. They were all on their knees and singing their KA sweetheart song. As you may know, it is a tradition for many fraternities to perform this ritual for the bride of their brother at weddings.

I did not fall asleep during this yoga session. Rather, I somehow then felt like I received a divine message. It was not an audible message. Nevertheless, if it were, it would be something like "Help me with Valentine's Day! Have my DTD brothers serenade my girls for Valentine's Day." Brilliant! It was Bob's first Valentine's Day away from his girls, and I was available to help Bob deliver gifts to them. I totally get it if that sounds strange because it was. But, it was a *good* strange to me.

I posted an old black and white photo of Bob on Facebook the previous day in honor of his daughter's fifth birthday. It was a photo of Bob when he was five. The caption read, "To Kiana From: Your Photo Crazy Aunt—This is your daddy when he was your age. Mimi and PaPa [our parents] later made a Christmas ornament out of his glasses [from the photo] and gave them to him a few years ago. He is looking down on you on your birthday." One of Bob's fraternity brothers saw this and direct messaged me that he wanted to have the brothers do something for Kiana's fifth birthday. (There's the #5 again.) Her birthday was on February 7, 2013.

I received that powerful message from Bob at yoga class; I realized that the brothers' gesture could either be a late fifth birthday gift or an on-time Valentine's Day gift for our niece. I wondered how we would be able to coordinate everything within seven days.

After yoga class, I ran to my car. It was about 9:00 am Florida time. Bob always made fun of me for forgetting the three-hour time difference when calling California. I was about to make that same mistake. I quickly Googled the closest university to Bob's family's home in California. I was happy to find that it was Stanford University. I then Googled the name of the President of the Delta Tau Delta House. It was a guy named Jacob.

Seconds later, I was talking to a groggy Jacob. I had no clue that he was a 250+-pound football player who was trying to sleep after having a typical late college night the previous day. It was 6:00 am California time, and I was excitedly telling my new friend Jacob about my epiphany. A few seconds into my explanation, I felt Bob remind me about the time difference. I apologized and asked Jacob if he could call me at his earliest convenience. Later that day, a more alert defensive-end football player kindly returned my call. He was such a great listener and seemed to understand Bob's story completely. I asked him if there was any way that he could recruit a few guys at the chapter meeting to serenade Nilufer & Kiana … on Valentine's Day.

Guess how many guys miraculously volunteered? Answer: 5

Meanwhile, Bob's University of Florida fraternity brother, Eric, was able to purchase a heart shaped locket from Tiffany's using funds that all of the old UF brothers had contributed. We had the locket mailed to Nilufer's neighbor's house days later.

Nilufer's niece Samira happened to be visiting her in California from the Orlando area that week. She would be there for Valentine's Day as well. (Thank God.) Poor Sam. Not knowing any other details, I was able to have her pick up the locket from the mail and insert a photo of Kiana and Bobby in it. I then remember asking her if she would be willing to meet five guys at a nearby gas station on Valentine's Day evening. She was dying to know why, but I did not reveal much else. I recall her asking me, "Please at least tell me if they are hot?" I explained that I did not even know them, which I am sure comforted her (sarcasm). Later, she told me that all five guys showed up on time and in their fraternity letters. Bobby is a clever one.

During the planning of what we began calling "Operation Secret Serenade," Jacob caved and told me how the fellas would be happy to help, but they don't really sing. Lol—I totally understood and wanted them to feel comfortable.

Do you remember Bob's Southwestern Books salesman and fraternity brother named Tony Carulli? Because pretty much everyone in that fraternity house had a nickname, he was always known by my family as "Rulli." Rulli realized that this moment would be a great opportunity for the fraternity's national magazine to cover. It could be a story about how fraternities are life-long and how the young and old members who did not even know each other and who were from opposite sides of the U.S. came together for this special Valentine's Day. We were able to have Sam delegate a family member from Nilufer and Sam's side of the family to be a photographer that evening (for whatever we were up to...). Those photos were used for the article below.

Nine months later, Rulli and Eric helped me to plan a one-year anniversary of Bob's passing where we unveiled this article on a plaque. It took place across the street from UF's football stadium at the DTD house. The young members graciously welcomed us. They served lunch and let us show a video about Bob and tell stories involving Bob in the living room. Bob's brothers from the 80s were full of entertaining stories. Rulli acted as the host/emcee. We did not know it at the time, but Rulli was living with esophageal cancer. Months later, he found out, told me about it, and remarked how he was "Not ready to see Bob yet." He lost his battle in March of 2016, approximately two and a half years after hosting Bob's UF memorial.

On Thursday, February 14, 2013, at 11:05:31 AM EST, Eric Criss wrote:

Gentlemen,

I just wanted to take a moment to make you aware that some of your ballplayers are doing a great thing for a 5-year-old little girl in Los Gatos. She lost her father, Bob Koechlin, recently when he was struck by a car while riding his bicycle. A group of his college buddies, myself included, and Bob's sister, Carolyn, bought Kiana a Tiffany locket for Valentine's Day and shipped it off to the family.

A few of your ballplayers, who also happen to be members of the Delta Tau Delta fraternity, are serenading this little girl and presenting her with the letter below when they give her the locket with a picture of she and her Daddy. They are doing this with no incentive other than it being a nice thing to do for a little girl and some Delt Fraternity brothers from Florida they never knew. Jacob at the Delt House is our point of contact. I just wanted you to know how grateful a big group of guys and a few girls are to this group of men at Stanford.

Here is the letter they are going to read to little Kiana:

Kiana,

You know your daddy loves the Gators, right? Well, you may or may not know that your daddy went to college at The University of Florida, where he made a lot of friends who call themselves his "Brothers." Well, I just want to tell you that his "Brothers" in Florida are friends with me (Jacob and name the rest of the guys present at the

Serenade) and my brothers at Stanford University right here in California. We are all "Brothers" and we all love our "Brothers" and everyone in our "Brothers' families." We are the "Brothers" of Delta Tau Delta, which might not mean anything to you now, but one day, I hope you will understand what it means.

We are here today to tell you that your Daddy loves you sooooo much that he made sure that all of us came here on Valentine's Day to sing/read to you and tell you that you will always be his special sweetheart! Kiana, since you are your daddy's sweetheart forever, you need to know that you will always be our sweetheart, too! Why? Because your daddy is "OUR BROTHER," and we want to help our "Brother" Bob Koechlin make this a very special day for you, Kiana, and for your mommy Nilufer too!

Guess what, Kiana? We have something for you that your daddy wanted us to give to you today…(present the gift)…This is a special necklace that has a pretty cool picture inside. (show her) OK, so every time you wear this or look at it, you will know that your daddy is always with you to protect you, make you happy and most of all, to make sure you know how much he loves you!

We hope you like it and want to wish you and your mom a Happy Valentine's Day from (Stanford Delt Chapter name at Stanford University) and our Brothers at Delta Zeta Chapter at the University of Florida…You both are officially our new Delta Tau Delta Sweethearts!

Regards,
Eric Criss
President
Beer Industry of Florida

Beta Rho Chapter Surprises Honorary Sweethearts

Robert Koechlin (University of Florida, 1989) was a man of many titles: adventurist, cyclist, philanthropist, Delt, brother and son; but the names he claimed most ardently were those of husband and father. Tragically Koechlin's life was cut short on Nov. 24, 2012 at the age of 45, and to honor his memory and his devotion to his family, five members of the Beta Rho Chapter surprised his wife and daughter with a heart-shaped Tiffany's locket and Valentine's Day serenade, naming them honorary Delta Tau Delta sweethearts.

Delta Zeta brothers, Eric Criss (University of Florida, 1991) and Tony Carulli (University of Florida, 1990), along with Koechlin's sister, Carolyn, were at the helm of the serenade surprise, which had to be planned and executed in little more than a week prior to Valentine's Day.

"The whole thing magically came together from beginning to end," said Carolyn.

Criss began collecting donations from Delta Zeta alumni to purchase the locket, while Carolyn called upon Jacob Gowan (Stanford University, 2013) and the Beta Rho Chapter in California to pitch the idea of having a group of brothers present the gift. Without hesitation, the Beta Rho Chapter jumped on board to participate in this tribute to a fallen brother.

"It was nice to give them some sort of comfort in this way," said Gowan. "It was a great way to spend our Valentine's Day."

Dan Nelsen, Miller Aaron, Alex Yazdi and Brendon Austin were in attendance along with Gowan to help make this Valentine's Day one to remember for the family of Brother Koechlin.

"We're in awe of what they did," said Carulli. "Those Stanford Delts were awesome."

Carulli drafted a letter to be read to Koechlin's daughter, Kiana, upon receiving the locket from the Beta Rho Delts. In the letter, which was read by Brother Aaron, Carulli wrote "Kiana, since you are your daddy's sweetheart forever, you need to know that you will always be our sweetheart, too."

More than 20 Delts from Florida and California were involved in making this inspiring idea a touching reality for Koechlin's wife and child.

"I've never experienced anything like this," said Carulli. "It was the true meaning of brotherhood."

> **❝ I've never experienced anything like this. It was the true meaning of brotherhood.**
> — Tony Carulli **❞**

Members of Beta Rho Chapter join the widow and daughter of Robert Koechlin for a special Delt Sweetheart presentation

CHAPTER 6

Bob's Journal

THE MONTH BEFORE Bob's accident, my parents visited him and his family in California. It was there that my parents were invited to a wedding on Nilufer's side of the family. (Remember the bear story? Parvin was to be the mother of the bride at this wedding.) After Bob passed, our father decided not to go to the wedding. My mom then asked me to take my dad's place on the flight from Tampa, Florida, to San Jose, California. I was very excited to go. While Bob was alive, we rarely saw him. After Bob's passing, our rate of travel to California seemed to have increased somehow.

The wedding took place on June 29, 2013. Counting the funeral, this was my second trip to California since the accident. I loved the comfort of having so many visitors during our trip there for the funeral. This visit was also special for the opposite reason: It was so quiet at Bob's house. I remember seeing his closets still full of his clothes, his bottle of Eternity for Men by the bathroom sink, an engraved Best Man flask from his buddy Warren, and the like.

The day of the wedding, Nilufer had to run errands for a few hours. I will always cherish that she suggested that my mom and I read through Bob's old journals while she was away. Bob had kept a journal through college and beyond. Nothing in the journals seemed ultra private. Out of respect for Bob, I will share the findings that I feel he would want us all to know and live by.

Most of what he wrote were motivational quotes about his goals and inspiring people that he had met.

In one of his journals, he talks about sunsets. Like many of us, Bob loved sunsets. In his journal, he mentioned something that I had not considered. He points out that most of the time, the best part of a sunset is after the sun has already set. The colors are amazing.

In another journal entry, he mentions waking up and being all-knowing and having new abilities. "Everyone I encountered would gain from the experience. Life would be perfect... I could walk on water, move through walls, and heal the sick..." Is this foreshadowing? I have depended on Bob so many times since his passing. Please help me to understand ___; please help my friends and family to get through yet another hurricane; please help me to use my gifts to help others. Did my brother's desire to use superpowers to help others translate to a stronger connection to us all once he ascended this mortal plane?

I left California, arrived back home in Florida, and got back to my routine, which involved attending a monthly Girl Scout Leaders' meeting. The meetings took place along the water at a church named Crystal Beach Community Church. Our meeting ended just as the sun was setting outside. I suppose that most meetings ended in the dark. Thus, I took the opportunity this one night to watch it set. I was standing there with my Girl Scout binders when this elderly lady walked up to me. She was short and holding a large camera to capture the beauty of the sky. She randomly leaned toward me and stated kinda softly, "You know, the best part of a sunset is after it has already set." Coincidence?

7/12 Wed

Tonight I'm wondering if there's a she who loves sunsets as much as I do. Maybe she wants to be left alone for a while. She believes that the world is a wonderful place, but she wants to make it better somehow(?) She is tired of rules, opinions, negative influences. She likes to dream, and she knows how to be happy. She wants to escape and chase her dream: chase sunsets! She wants a friend. She wants to be different, and she wants to learn as well as teach, and, most of all, wonder, "Where's my wondering partner?" she asks the sunset. She finds her reply in the wind, the clouds, the sky, and the moon. And you know what? I'm asking the same question and getting the same reply. "…Patience," says the sky. "Keep dreaming, hoping, wondering. Create her for yourself. Draw her into your life. But don't forget me and the beach, the clouds, the stars, and the moon. We'd miss you so. Please don't forget." How could I forget things so beautiful? They're the only things that are real.

Buy a surfboard

What if one day I woke up and all of a sudden I had every answer to any question I could think of asking. Not only that, but I had seen through the illusions of the world. I knew how to make myself happy whenever I wanted to be happy, excited when I wished to be excited, brave when I needed to be brave. I litterally was in control of my entire life; every aspect of it. If I wanted to be rich by the end of the day, an idea would pop into my head and the methods to use to get there.

I could even walk on water, move through walls, and heal the sick; especially if the sick was me. It would take no time at all to learn to fly; just hop into any airplane and go. I would immediately work my body into shape. I would materialize jet skis and airplanes and beach homes. No need for currency when you can materialize anything you want right there on the spot. I would never be boring or conceited or greedy. I would be the best boyfriend imaginable and my friends would be as happy as I. I could establish rapport instantly with anyone I chose, and everyone I encountered would gain from the

> experience. Life would be perfect. No
> crime, no real death, no bribery or
> stealing or murder. Just fun, bliss,
> excitement, and extasy. No disease.
>   My work wouldn't be work at
> all because I would love to do it.
> People would pay me and I would
> laugh. I would never be tired
> until it was time for bed and
> then I could experiment w/ out of
> body experiences and dream states
> and different planes of consciousness.
> The next morning I would pop out
> of bed, utterly excited to see what
> the day had in store. I could eat
> as much as I want and never get
> fat.

What if one day I woke up and all of a sudden I had every answer to any question I could think of asking? Not only that, but I had power over the illusions of the world. I knew how to make myself happy whenever I wanted to be happy, excited when I wished to be excited, brave when I needed to be brave. I literally was in control of my entire life, every aspect of it. If I wanted to be rich by the end of the day, an idea would pop into my head and the methods to use to get there.

I could even walk on water, move through walls, and heal the sick; especially if the sick was me. It would take no time at all to learn to fly; just hop into any airplane and go. I could immediately work my body into shape. I could materialize jet skis and airplanes and beach homes. No need for currency when you can materialize anything you want right there on the spot. I would never be boring or conceited or greedy. I would be the best boyfriend imaginable, and my friends would be as happy as I. I could establish rapport instantly with anyone I chose, and everyone I encountered would gain from the experience.

2nd page:

Life would be perfect. No crime, no real death, no bribery or stealing or murder. Just fun, bliss, excitement, and ecstasy. No disease.

My work would not be work at all because I would love to do it. People would pay me, and I would laugh. I would never be tired until it was time for bed, and then I could experiment with out-of-body experiences and dream states and different planes of consciousness. The next morning, I would pop out of bed, utterly excited to see what the day had in store. I could eat as much as I wanted and never get fat.

CHAPTER 7

A Stronger Family

ALTHOUGH WE ALL loved Bob, I think that most of our friends and family members would agree that losing him has made most of us stronger.

Nilufer had a forest planted in Bob's name in Tahoe through the Sugar Pine Foundation. Bob's ski group in Stowe, Vermont, created a ski trail called "Bob's Rash," which actually has nothing to do with a rash. Read on for the origin…

The Legend of Hot Music
Shared by Eric Santini on December 28, 2012

Many people have asked if the "snow potion" that Nilufer spoke of is actually true. While the actual recipe is somewhat shrouded in mystery and folklore at this point, and quite complicated if I remember correctly, the answer is yes, yes, yes. It started as a snow dance, which then morphed into a questionable concoction that no one is proud of. Nilufer recently asked if I had the actual recipe/ingredients, and in my search for the original manuscript, it brought back another funny, wonderful, priceless memory of Bob up at Stowe, Vermont.

It was actually the very first time I met Bob. It was maybe the 2nd or 3rd week of the "Ski Haus," 1996-ish. Bob had recently moved to Boston, and our mutual friend, Lisa, was the only one Bob knew in the area. Lisa invited Bob up to the Ski Haus to introduce him to everyone and enjoy the winter.

Bob, of course, did not hesitate to blindly walk into our little clique and win us over. I remember the first night he walked in. All he had with him was a small overnight bag, the clothes on his back, and a leather Top Gun aviator jacket.

Well, as the night grew old, someone asked Bob if he was skiing with us in the morning. Of course, Bob had never skied before, but we didn't know this at the time. His answer was filled with eagerness. "I don't know, maybe, I guess, maybe, ok, I'll do it!"

We asked Bob where his gear was, and he replied he didn't have any. We asked, "What about a jacket?" and he replied, "I have my leather coat."

"What!!! You can't ski in a leather jacket!"

"You came to Vermont in January with no coat?!!??"

We gave Bob so much crap about that for years on end. We never let him forget that, but that is just where the story begins: the legend of the Hot Music jacket was born.

That night, we scrambled to get Bob at least the minimum gear he needed to survive a winter day in Vermont. We were failing miserably when someone opened a coat closet just off the kitchen. I can remember it like it was yesterday. There it was. The only thing in the closet. The Hot Music jacket was just perfect. Now, close your eyes and imagine the worst 1980s, neon, Miami Vice-looking ski jacket you can come up with. Well, you would be wrong. It was worse, way worse; the entire inside of the coat had "Hot Music" stitched all through it. Not to mention, it was a women's coat. A very petite woman's coat that someone had left there from the year before, no doubt on purpose. I can't even type this without laughing my butt off. This would be Bob's crucible. If he could handle this, he would be one of us.

Bob not only handled it, he wore it proudly. The sleeves were too short, and he could barely zip it up. It was beautiful. I remember a large group of us were skiing a barely known, kinda out-of-bounds trail called The River Bed. In the summer it is actually a river that freezes over in the winter and creates a quite difficult run. This might have been Bob's third day skiing…maybe….if that. Bob had no business being on that trail, but we all know how Bob handled any challenge. We all got to the bottom and were standing there in a small circle when we noticed Bob was missing. Oops, maybe we shouldn't have brought him in here, but no one ever accused us of being the brightest bunch. That's when we saw him. Somehow, he had made his way off to skier's right and was crashing through the trees completely out of control. Arms waving above his head. His weight leaning too far to the left and then back to the right. The glorious Hot Music coat unzipped and blowing in the wind. He was coming at us fast, and we all started to nervously back up. Just then, at the very last second, he face-planted and bit it right at our feet. "Bob, are you ok?" we all asked, 97% laughing and 3% really kinda concerned. Bob looked up with the biggest grin you can imagine. "We have to do that again!" he cried.

"Of course, we'll do it again, and you can take that foolish jacket off now; you earned it. Oh, and remember, there are NO friends on a powder day."

P.S. And yes, the snow potion works. Bob made it snow three straight weeks. I wonder what ever happened to that Hot Music jacket.

Later, Eric shared that another time while skiing in Vermont, Bob yelled to his buddies, "I have a rash." He was actually telling them that he had to rest. However, the friends liked the first version better.

After Bob passed, Nilufer shared some of his ashes with this close ski group. They had a few shots out of a plastic iguana before nailing a pink (in honor of the pink, Hot Music jacket) license plate to a tree that read, "Bob's Rash." I am told that skiers have since assumed that the sign (get it: sign!) signified the beginning of an unofficial trail. Thus, it has now become a worn-in trail so that others can share in the joy of Bob's Rash.

Last run of the day down the Bruce Trail to
Matterhorn to celebrate Bah-Card-Dee..

In the summer of 2018, I had a girls' weekend with my Dunedin High School friends in the Stowe, Vermont, area. They were so kind as to go on a hunt with me for the pink sign. Bob's pals usually go there during the winter. I FaceTimed one of them to see if he could help me locate it. However, with all of the greenery, it became challenging. After over an hour of looking, my friends and I decided to pop a bottle of champagne in a creek because we had gotten close enough. I think that Bob was there in spirit and that he may have even grown some of the lush flowers and shrubs that we saw that summer. I picked a few yellow flowers in that area and pressed them for Nilufer and Kiana. I found out later that many curious skiers in Stowe noticed the pink sign in the white snow and took the out-of-bounds trail. It was just a spot in the woods prior to the birth of the sign. It's another sign!

Kiana seems to be a happy girl and is athletic like Bob.

In July of 2012, before Bob had passed, I sent my bent Thule bike rack back to the Trek store in Clearwater to have it fixed. They then sent it to Thule in Seymour, Connecticut. I checked its status a few times over a four-month period to see when it would be ready. Progress was not being made. Upon my return from Bob's funeral, I received a message from the store that the bike rack was magically ready. It could have shipped on his last day here.

As I was leaving the Trek store with the repaired bike rack, I saw a large calendar on a whiteboard within the store near the front door. It read, "Ride of Silence (ROS) on May 15, 2013." I inquired about it with a store employee. The staff guided me to the International Ride of Silence webpage, where it explained that the event takes place worldwide at 7 pm one day every May. The participants ride 10 miles in silence to honor those who have passed in a cycling accident and to bring awareness to automobile drivers to share the road. I immediately shared the site with my siblings as I knew that they may want to participate in their home cities. My little brother Matt rode in the Dunedin, Florida, ROS, our older sister Mary and her family rode in the Atlanta/Alpharetta, Georgia, one, and our oldest sibling Kathleen rode the one in Columbus, Ohio. The tradition was a new one. It was exciting to participate in it wearing Bob's cycling shirt.

Another incident that happened since my new intuition kicked in after Bob passed involves stories like this one:

I am sending this to a select few friends whom I feel will understand. I can't keep this information to myself because I get so much hope from these things that keep happening.

A few nights ago, Chris, Rees, and I began preparing her goodie bags for her surfing party. As some of you know, they involved a coconut stuffed with a bag of jelly beans/drink umbrella. The first step was to drain the coconuts. The second step was to drain the juice with a coffee filter to separate the brown shell matter from it (so that we could make coconut ice cubes for Homer smoothies after the party.) We have a Keurig. Hence, we do not have coffee filters. That night, it wasn't until we knocked on the third neighbor's door (Carol's) that we found someone home who had the filters that we needed. We told her that it was for a project and we thanked her. As we walked home, I told Rees that I hoped we would have one goodie bag left over after the party so we could give it to her as another thank you.

The party happened on Sunday. Sunday night, while dressed in PJs that my mom gave me (that said "Peace, Love, Coffee") and Hawaiian pants, I felt the urge to follow through with my idea. Rees was sleeping. The extra coconut was sitting on my counter, staring at me. For some reason, I had to take it to the neighbor Carol, although it was nearly 9 pm.

While walking to their door, ready to explain my outfit to them, I said to my brother Bob jokingly, "Love thy neighbor." I knocked twice. I knew they were home because a light was on. Figuring they thought I was probably out of my mind and did not want to answer, I left the item at the door and went home. I immediately texted my neighbor, Melissa, at 8:48 pm, saying, "Do u have a # or e-mail for neighbors across from you? We have something for them. Thanks." Then, I got on my Yahoo account. As I was doing this, three ambulances started flashing their lights down the street and up to Carol's house. My e-mail to Melissa read,

> *"Melissa,*
>
> *>>*
>
> *>> Random question: Can I get the e-mail address for the neighbors in the house across the street from you? I left something outside their house and want to make sure they know why. Now I see the ambulances there. Yikes. I hope that everything is okay with her father.*
>
> *>>*
>
> *>> Thank you,*
>
> *>> Carolyn"*

(Sadly, I had forgotten Carol's name.) Carol had been taking care of her father there for about one year. After learning of his death from Melissa, I went to

Carol's home. I told Carol my story above and then showed her my e-mail from 8:48 pm, wondering if that was his time of death. It was.

Just before our daughter began her freshman year of high school, I volunteered to help with an alumni reunion. The parent in charge asked me if I could take a cart to the cafeteria and go upstairs to gather vases for the tables. While looking for the vases, I noticed a stack of old newspapers on a table near the vases. The issue on the top was from just prior to 1985. Knowing that was Bob's graduating year (at that same school), I had to open it. What I next saw was a photo of my brother with a quote regarding what he is thankful for: "I am thankful for all of my friends at CCC and for the religious atmosphere which allows me to grow spiritually and morally. Most of all, I am thankful for photosynthesis because, without it, we would not be what we are today. – Bob Koechlin" The photosynthesis bit was sarcastic. I know this because we all went around the table at Thanksgiving and read what we were thankful for. Bob went on and on about photosynthesis when it was his turn. I have a copy of this letter, but it is buried in storage.

After I saw the old newspaper, I knew this was the school for our daughter and that Uncle Bobby would watch over all of the malarkey, which gave me both peace and a bit of worry. Either way, there Bob was looking at me.

Speaking of our daughter, she had just (JUST) started her freshman year at Florida State University. Many things there are competitive and in high demand, including housing. Relieved that the classes, finances, et cetera, were finally in motion, I received a call at my desk while at work. Our daughter was panicked about apartments for THE FOLLOWING SCHOOL YEAR, which were already being reserved. It was time to sign a lease already for the sophomore year at FSU. Neither she nor I was ready for this. She and her friends were going from apartment to apartment, trying to find housing that was not already snagged.

After approximately the fourth stop, she texted me. She was frustrated. I replied, "Jesus knows what it is like to have no room in the inn. Keep the faith. Look for a sign from Uncle Bobby."

Flashback to the late 1970s. Bob would have been approximately twelve years old when "Rapper's Delight" was released. There are many versions of the song. Its length varies from approximately 4 minutes to approximately 14 minutes. I am not sure which version Bobby memorized back then, but it was long. For 40+ years, every time I hear that song, I think of Bob. Our daughter had been told this story and knew the song.

Back to 2023, it was, I believe, day two of apartment hunting for our daughter. While at work, she texted that she received her sign, followed by an actual sign in the model unit of an apartment near campus that happened to have space for our daughter and her friends. The words on the sign were lyrics from the chorus of "Rapper's Delight."

We'll take it!

Around the time of Bob's passing, our sister Kathleen had taken on a love of cycling. What started out as a routine of riding her bike to work has become a very serious hobby where she has traveled as far as 100+ miles with her cycling group. She now leads hundreds of cyclists every May in Columbus, Ohio's Ride of Silence. Oftentimes, she is interviewed on the local news about it. She even had a bike tattooed onto her arm involving Bob's initials.

Oldest sister Kathleen's tattoo in honor of Bob

Our sister Mary and her husband opened up their very own sign store in November of 2016. Coincidence? Also, an interesting opportunity fell into the sign company's lap a few years later. One day, HGTV approached the sign company to see if they would like to participate in a show featuring designer Anitra Mecadon and rapper Lil Jon. The next thing we knew, they were on national TV via the show *Lil Jon Wants to Do What?*

Our parents are troopers and have also made the most of our circumstances. Bob is probably proud to know that our dad began a workout routine for the first time in his life. Dad participated in a CrossFit class with his older brother (our Uncle Tom) for several years until Uncle Tom reached the age of 91. Uncle Tom is now with Bobby up there somewhere, looking down on us all. I hope to be as active as my father and his brother were in their older years.

Our mom tries to encourage us to participate/initiate a random act of kindness on Bobby's birthday. She also usually has flowers presented in his honor at mass in town on each of his birthdays since he has passed.

On Bobby's birthday in 2021, Mom got the intuition/urge to reach out to an old neighbor who used to live across the street from my childhood home (and where my parents still live today). The neighbor's name was Donna. Donna had three teens when they lived near us. That house was always active. Donald was the oldest son living there. He and his brother Chris began working for Outback Steakhouse at an early age. Outback had its headquarters in nearby Tampa. This convenience allowed Donald and Chris to climb the ladder and continue working for Outback for many years as adults. Donald ended up taking a job for Outback in Honolulu, Hawaii. I was friends with the youngest sibling, Carol-Lynn. She was in many beauty pageants. All three of the teens kept Mom Donna very busy.

Less than three years after Bobby had passed, we found out that Donald passed away on June 5, 2015, from a heart attack in Honolulu. Like Bobby, he passed away at the age of 45 and left behind a young child. My Mom knew about this story. Guided by her intuition, she reached out to Donna to connect for the first time in decades. Mom did not have Donna's number but knew where she lived. So she left Donna a note (on paper) reaching out to see if Donna might be interested in having coffee at the nearby Kahwa coffee location. The two connected at Kahwa and caught up on years of life. Donna passed unexpectedly less than five months later, on January 18, 2022.

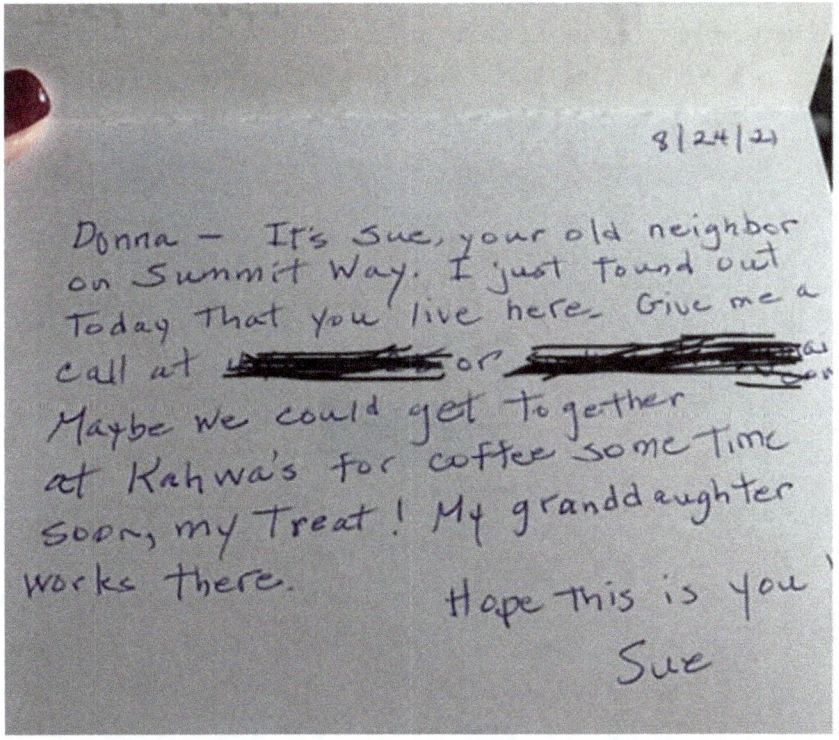

Thank God I still have at least one brother and my two sisters. Our youngest sibling, Matt, is now the only brother here. Bob was a big part of his life, and he dealt with his passing differently than I did. (We actually all handled the grief differently among our family members.) Perhaps for this reason, it took Matt a little longer than me to see Bob's signs. Eventually, it happened. I am glad that it did because I have always wanted Matt to experience the signs that we have all been witnessing for years. Matt still strives to maintain this brotherly connection and live each day inspired by Bob's philosophy of life.

Many of Bob's loved ones still feel his presence and experience winks and nods from him. Now that I have taken notice, signs appear from my brother frequently. Before Rulli also passed, Rulli and I would oftentimes discuss how Bob was helping us here. Now that Rulli is gone, I only feel closer to them both. I do have to make a conscious effort to communicate with them. However, when I do, I truly believe that they are listening, and that gives me peace.

CHAPTER 8

Come Sail Away Revisited

Styx coincidentally arrived in our hometown for a concert just after
I initially connected with the publishers of this book.

WHILE SEARCHING FOR jobs on LinkedIn in 2023, I noticed an acquaintance, Jessica, from high school, mentioning how she and a fellow Dunedin Falcon graduate, Laura, had started a publishing company. I reached out to the two of them before Christmas to tell them about the book idea and to see if they could help me get my act together to finally get this ball rolling. They seemed to understand the concept and how it really did not come from me but rather was born the day that my brother died. During this Zoom call, Jessica mentioned how she lived in the Clearwater Beach area.

After chatting with Laura and Jessica, I was led to Styx's site. The band has been a band for over 50 years, so the members are now about 70 years old. I was simply checking out their website. The first piece of information on their site was that their next show was on January 5, 2024 (of course, it was a five again!), in Clearwater, Florida, and basically in Jessica's backyard. They were playing at a newly renovated venue that I had been wanting to visit, and the tickets were only $40. My intuition kicked in. I told Jessica that this basically fell in my lap and that I felt like I was supposed to take her to the show. She was up for it, so I bought tickets. After choosing general admission/lawn seats, the venue sent a receipt showing that it had given us seats 227 and 228. 227? Really? Remember, this was the timestamp on his iPod where "Come Sail Away" had paused.

A few days passed, and Jessica checked in with me. She mentioned how she had the concert on her calendar but that if I had any siblings who might want her ticket, "by all means." I had mentioned to Jess and Laura on our Zoom call how all of my siblings lived in different states. I was the only one living in our hometown near our parents. Why would Jess think that I could easily take a sibling to this concert?

During quiet time (I always think best during moments of silence), I realized that our oldest sibling would be in town after the new year, which happened to be the week of the concert. I called her while on a bike ride to our folks' house. "I know that we have spoken about Styx and Bob's accident, but do you actually like the band?" I asked. "Styx was my first concert when I was 17," said my sister in her late 50s. What? Jessica happily gave Kathleen her ticket and started to understand the concept of Bob's signs, for she had just been a part of one.

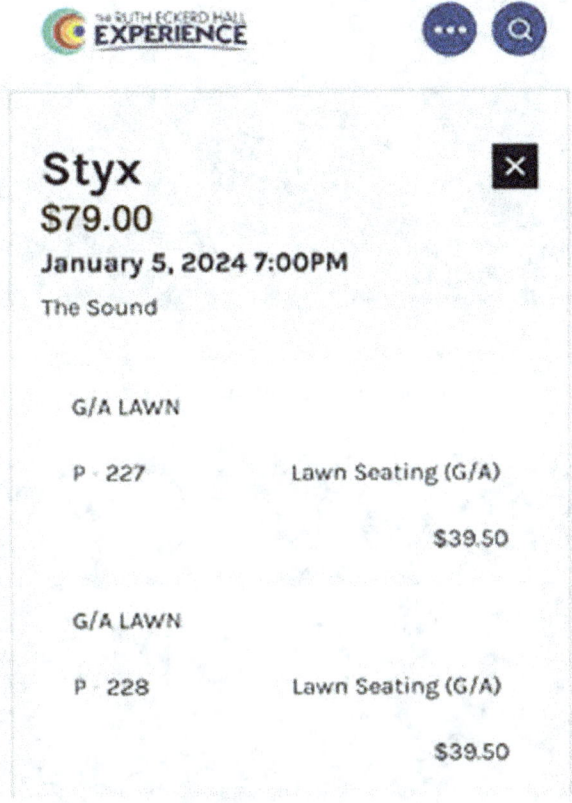

A stranger offered to take this family photo for us on Clearwater Beach.
The sun is sending a ray of light through Bob's daughter, Kiana.

This memorial appeared in Truckee at the roundabout after Bob's passing.

CHAPTER 9

Bob Completes His Book on a DHS Girls' Vacation

As MENTIONED BRIEFLY previously, about 5 of my Dunedin High School/college/ sorority friends (there's a lot of overlap) and I try to take annual summer reunion trips. In 2023, they voted on Napa Valley, which was funny because Nilufer has a house there. We ended up renting her house for the trip. It was along a vineyard and was fabulous.

In 2024, they had voted on Truckee, California. Calling it Tahoe, they actually chose a house on Donner Lake in Truckee, California. I was all in because this is where Bob took his last breath and earned (what my parents call) his eternal reward. Because I know that Bob is OK, I am completely OK with this town. I had taken a "get me out of this COVID shutdown" trip there with our daughter in 2020 and had already seen the roundabout. It is in a beautiful, peaceful area that I would not mind visiting many times.

So, out of all the places in the world for our next girls' reunion trip, my friends decided to rent an Airbnb a few minutes away from the roundabout where Bob's accident happened. As I was in the packing phase for the trip, my mom realized that we would be there for (what would have been) Bob's 57th birthday. Although it was probably awkward for my pals, they agreed that we could honor Bobby on his birthday by visiting the roundabout.

The morning of Bob's birthday was freaking cold. Five of us on the trip had started this trip departing from Florida for Truckee, where Florida had a feels like temperature of 100 degrees or so. I am not a huge fan of humid heat and welcomed the idea of having less humid, colder weather on this trip. But on Bob's birthday, it was in the 30s!

Mornings in Truckee were fun. We all had coffee together and chatted about current events. On the Saturday of the trip (our first full day there and Bob's birthday), our one pal, Ansley, suggested that we all do a yoga video before getting ready for the day. Renee was in the back of our little living room session and could see a rainbow forming out of the dining area's bay windows. Remaining respectful of the peace and serenity involved in our session, she kept her mouth shut until the end. "You guys, there is a rainbow! I did not want to interrupt yoga, but it's been here for a few minutes." We all excitedly left the house to see

it in our PJs on the back porch. It went across Donner Lake and seemed to be getting slightly larger and brighter every 10 minutes or so. I went back inside and sent my friends photos from our trip to California when Bob's daughter (four years old at the time) noticed a double rainbow outside of her front door. Flash forward to 2024, and a double rainbow started forming above our Donner Lake one. Although the second one stayed faint, I got Bob's memo. It was his birthday, and he was showing off again. I love it when that happens.

My friends and I then watched the Florida State game that was being played in Ireland, canceled our WHITEWATER RAFTING TRIP (lol—Floridians), and got dressed for the cold day. We started off in Palisades, Olympic Valley, to shop. It was a rainy day, but we did the best we could. I found out later that day that Nilufer met Bob in Palisades, previously known as Squaw Valley.

Although awkward and still raining, we were to pass Bob's roundabout on the way home … on his birthday. My friends took one for the team, parked the car (no, minivan) near the roundabout, walked in the rain, and paid tribute. I wanted them to be in the photo with me so that we could send it to my mom. I told them that it was ok to smile, but a few of them did not feel that was appropriate. That's OK. They were just being respectful, which also made for some ironically amusing photos of half-smiling/half-kinda-mourning. We then went to a nearby historical house/bar and had an official toast to Bob. Capping the day off with "Alexa" playing all of our favorites, mainly 90s songs, made for the perfect day. "Good Vibrations" by Marky Mark is always a fan favorite. I left that trip wondering if this was the final chapter of this book that Bob was helping me to write. The sand is moving through the hourglass. It would be fabulous to present this to my folks before they depart us for Bob, if that is how this life is going to go. I am depending on divine intervention here as I am not an author.

So, all of these signs began with receiving the one sign the second that our brother passed. I had to use intuition and seek out a way to communicate with Bob in order to see and feel all of these "coincidences." I feel that he enjoys keeping in touch with us. I hope that this book enables you to make the most of your new relationship with your loved ones who have passed. If you get any signs and want to share them with the world, please post your stories to www.heaven227.com. For now, we receive the signs, and perhaps later, we will be the givers of them. God bless!

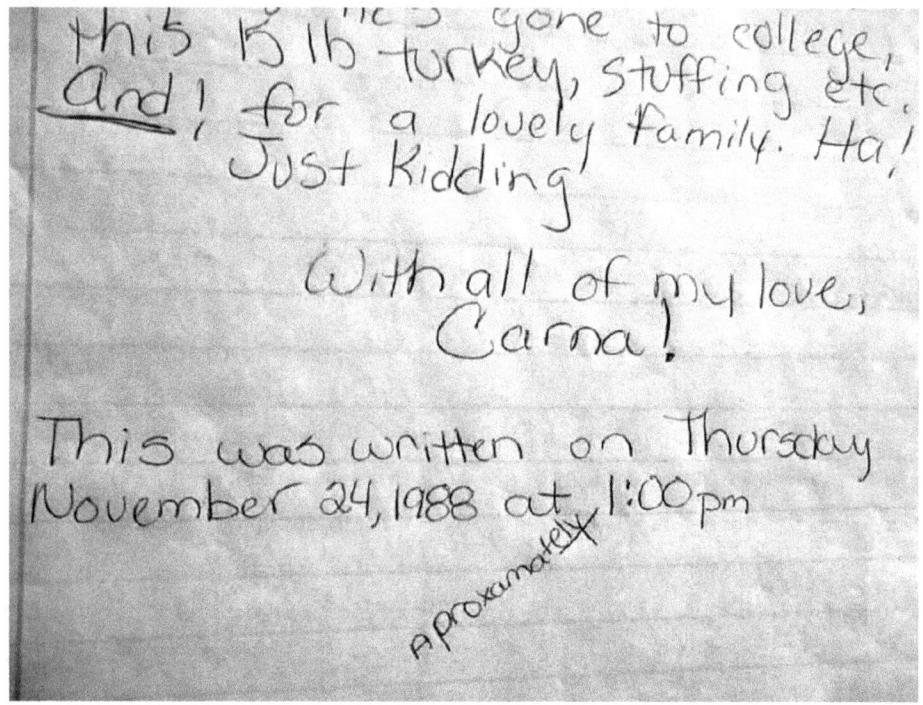

I found this note at the bottom of a Thanksgiving message. I wrote down the date and time, not knowing that 24 years later, it would be the end of Bob's dash.

Acknowledgments

Nilufer Koechlin for sharing the police report that opened my eyes to hope beyond this life

My parents for tolerating our hectic household, being our rocks, and teaching us about faith

My husband and daughter for putting up with my reactions to Bob's signs all of these years

Dunedin High School's Mrs. Bytheway for teaching us writing skills that we all use daily, and Dunedin High School's Wildebeest Publishing Company

The Delta Tau Delta brothers of the University of Florida and Stanford University for showing us that brotherhood is actually more than a lifelong commitment

Everyone who shared stories and photos about Bob back in 2012 when we had no idea how to handle all of this

The band Styx for writing such a timeless song… May a gathering of angels sing a song of hope to us all.

A Place for Jotting Down Signs

_____

_____

_____

_____

_____

_____

_____

_____

_____

_____

_____

About the Author

Carolyn Homer is a Floridian who considers herself very lucky to have grown up in the 1980s before technology took over the world. She loved growing up Koechlin as the fourth of five children.

She earned an undergraduate degree from the University of Florida and an MBA from the University of South Florida. She married Florida native Chris Homer. They have one daughter, who is a fifth-generation Homer from Pinellas County.

It was never her goal to write a book. However, she knew that it was one of her brother Bob's goals and used her intuition to guide her through this process.